the WOLF PACK MOON

Richard Rensberry

Copyright © 2015 by Richard Rensberry

All rights reserved. First printed in 2015.

ISBN-13 (eBook): 978-1-940736-07-5
ISBN-13 (Trade Paperback): 978-1-940736-06-8

In accordance with the U.S. Copyright Act of 1976, the scanning, uploading, and electronic sharing of any part of this book without permission of the publisher constitute unlawful piracy and theft of the author's intellectual property. No part of this book may be reproduced or transmitted in any form or by any means, electronic or mechanical, including photocopying, recording, or by any information storage and retrieval system, except for excerpts used for reviews, without permission in writing from the publisher.

Cover design by Bri Bruce, Bri Bruce Productions
Cover artwork by Richard Rensberry

Published by QuickTurtle Books®

For more information, visit www.richardrensberry.com

This book is dedicated to those with the courage to keep the lights on and shining bright. The future has no boundaries but those by which our thoughts are bound.

April 7, 2015, on the birthday of my lovely wife and muse, Mary.

May love guide the planets and steer the stars. Have a good one.

CONTENTS

Preface i
Acknowledgements iii
The Gamble 1
The Sentinel 3
If I Were . . . 5
Wounded 7
Stoned and Depressed 9
Bully 11
The Big House 13
Security 15
Mother and Father 17
Ecology 19
Mountain Boat 21
The Past 23
Justice 27
My Enemies 29
Lost and Found 31
High Hopes 33
The Universe 35
Noah's Arc 37
Handshake 39
If I Were Done 41
Fire 43
Social Mania 45
Morning Commute 47
Dirty Words 49
Pretty Tight Buns 51
Voice 53
Food for Thought 55
The Key 57
Wolf Pack Moon 59

Home **61**
Touch and Grace **63**
Respite **65**
Under the Weather **67**
Ghost **69**
A Habit Good **71**
Heaven **73**
The Pantry **75**
A Grape Poet **77**
The Rock **79**
The End **81**
Afterword **83**

Preface

The lion's share of these poems was written under the spell of the *wolf pack moon* during the months of January and February 2015. This is the name given to the moon phase by the Algonquin Indians that hunted and gathered in the Great Lakes region of North America where I spent my youth wandering in their footsteps.

I have always maintained a great affinity for the spirit with which our Native American ancestors conducted their lives. Their reverence for the landscape within and the landscape without is a lesson well served for future generations.

We do not live on a sterile rock, we live on a living and breathing planet that is multi-dimensional and interdependent. We cannot survive alone as a human species. We survive with the help and magic of a myriad of other species that coexist alongside us.

I am not all that conversant with astrology, but I do know that the moon and the planets have a direct and indirect impact on life and the physical universe. Would I have written the same poetry under the influence of a *strawberry moon* or a *harvest moon*? Not very likely. So, I give to you the wolf pack poems. I believe that they are straightforward and modern. I made no attempts to disguise myself within the words.

Acknowledgements

I would like to thank Bri Bruce for her help in bringing this book to fruition. Her editing, cover design and book layout were done with care. I would also like to thank my wife, Mary, for her love and companionship in this great quest to keep our planet intact for future generations to come. None of us can go it alone and as they say in the game of poker, I'm all in.

the WOLF PACK MOON

Richard Rensberry

The Gamble

If I were luck,
I'd choose to be good.
I'd live in your pocket
and kiss your fingers
long before you rolled the dice.
I'd blow on your hands and help you out
with a flippant flip of a silver coin. If I were luck,
I'd pick from the deck
the ace of hearts. You'd hit the jackpot
of love and friendship. We'd trick the devil
and outwit gods. If I were luck,
you'd beat the odds.

The Sentinel

If I were a redwood,
I'd stand on a mountain shrouded in fog.
I'd be the tallest and grandest of all.
Eagles would come
to perch on my arms, crows would caw
in vigilance. Wings would fold
to nurture their young,
safe from the edge of tines and tongues.
If I were a redwood, I'd converse with the moon
and kiss the stars. I'd sway
in the wind and begin each day
with a dawn painted purple and red. I'd be humbled
by God and the miracle of song
composed and sung by wrens. I'd bend
to the rhythm of tumultuous storms and move
with the stealth of paws. If I were a redwood,
I'd huddle in the rain and cling to the cliffs
of granite and schist that hold me. I'd be sentinel
to preciousness, beauty, and peace. I'd live
far beyond the logger's reach of saws and lack
of benevolence. If I were a redwood,
I'd live in the throes of heavenly bliss
in the northern coastal wilderness.

IF I WERE . . .

If I were a poem,
I'd seek to inspire
while striking a match.
I'd set words on fire.
I'd make them smolder
and hiss in the dark,
crackle, and spark.
They'd whorl like comets
and twinkle like stars.
They'd lick like flames
at the Devil's hearth.

If I were a poem,
I'd preach from the fire
beside nuns and drunks
a Saint and a liar.
I'd mix recipes
to bake in your head
like wit and rhyme
in a loaf of bread.
You'd think of times
all torn apart.
If I were a poem,
I'd wring your heart.

Wounded

If I were hit,
the medics would
put me back together
with duct tape and titanium screws.
I'd be wearing slightly used artillery boots.
If I were hit, bright red would drip
monotonous as the chaplain's prayer, confirmation
that pessimism was far from scarce. If I were hit,
I'd hear metal on metal
and metal on bone, voices
like those of a devil. I'd sense my friends believing in blood
and viscera. They'd watch the knife
fillet and slice as my nerves are rendered
deaf and dumb to the percussion of a mechanical lung.
If I were hit I'd feel squeezed and rung
completely out. What I would crave most
is a beer, the cold wet sweat
of the bottle and the bitter
bite, the later buzz of laughter as someone tells
a dirty joke. If I were hit, I'd lean over the fence
in the backyard. I'd smell the aromas
from my neighbor's pit
and relish the roasting of something other
than me.

STONED AND DEPRESSED

If I were a drug,
I'd be a hipster, I'd be a trickster, I'd be an imp.
I'd tickle you.
I'd mess with your head. I'd stare you down
and win. If I were a drug, I'd be hostile
with a smile. I'd make you cringe. I'd make you laugh
with a syringe in the palm of your hand.
I'd be a demon, I'd be a punk. I'd be a brother
and a sister and a drunk without compassion, without remorse.
I'd remember, I'd forget. I'd stink, I'd lie, I'd cheat.
If I were a drug,
I'd be the epitome of deceit.

BULLY

If I were an onion,
I'd get in your face.
I'd take your breath
and give you mine.
I'd burn your heart
and spit in your eye.
If I were an onion,
I'd make you cry.

The Big House

If I were San Quentin,
I would hold the key
to everything evil.
My heart would beat
with the tattooed fists
of men sentenced
into my keep, boys gone
crazy as their crimes.
I'd feel like guilt
most of the time. I'd be a maze
of whispers and lies. Truth,
if it existed at all, would arrive
in shackles, whimper and fold
on death row.
I'd have rats for eyes.
I would hold you close
and gnaw on your will. Time
would stagger, stumble and fall
still as their victims.
If I were San Quentin,
I'd have an IQ
of ten. I'd clatter and clank
the whole night through.
I'd hone my shank
and lower my pants.

Richard Rensberry

I'd show you the sorriest
crack of an ass
if I were San Quentin.

Security

If I were a window,
I'd be invisible to wings.
Flies would buzz
and head-bang bees. Wasps
would sting. Gnats
I'd knock unconscious. I'd be clearly
clean of guilt. If I were a window,
it would be my duty
to keep the buggers out.

Mother and Father

If I were the rain,
I would be less begrudging.
I'd teach Heaven how to beat
a rhythmical drum. I would
speak fluent and decisive electricity. I'd strike up
a conversation with the wind
and babble with the trees and roofs. If I were the rain,
I'd hammer away as if I could play
the piano like Jerry Lee.
I'd fill large buckets. I'd gorge the streams.
I'd purge the skies with claps of thunder
If I were the rain. I'd be anxious to please.
I'd be the crescendo in a symphony choir.
I'd be mother and father to the land and seas.

ECOLOGY

If I were a tree,
I'd be firmly rooted
to Mother Earth.
My limbs would reach
with delicate hands
and extended fingers.
I would pray for you.

I'd collect the sun
in palmate buckets. I would
give to you a pool
of deep shade
to have your family
picnic. You could
spread a blanket and stay
the whole day through.

I'd invite the breeze.
You could listen and snooze
to the bumble of bees.
A brook would chortle.
Larks would sing. I'd have
fruit to bear
amidst the wintergreen
if I were a tree.

RICHARD RENSBERRY

We could sit in peace
and tranquility, discuss specifics
on how to build
a community, call it
Oak Grove or Apple Creek,
Cedar Village or Maple Lane. You
would nod your head
and wipe your brow, rub your chin
and put down your pen, propose
to keep me as I am, if
I were a tree.

Mountain Boat

If I were a lake,
I'd hide in the mountains. I'd be pure
as the springs that feed me.
I'd be harbor to willow, aspen,
and birch. I would
frame your cabin in majestic firs
or red cedar. If I were a lake,
you could look beyond all worry. I would
give you vision behind your head.
I'd make everything sparkle
If I were a lake. You could
swim in my body
or think in my head; you could
immerse yourself but you wouldn't drown.
If I were a lake, I'd flood your heart
and float your boat away.

The Past

I

If I were the past,
I'd be in Northern Michigan. I'd be in the birch
and beech forest where it meets the river.
I'd be in the river where it meets the open
waters of Lake Superior. I'd smell the thaw
and the burgeoning rush of spring.
I'd feel the bluster of wind whistling
out of Canada from Alaska, the subtle tug and pull
of a steelhead at the end of my rod. If I were the past,
I would be turning sod near the rhubarb. I'd be preparing
green peas and tomatoes, beans, radishes, and chives
to eat with the trout. I'd kick back in the swing
with a beer at dusk. The neighbors would call. The black bats
would fall from the folds of the patio umbrella and squeal
for the night.
The lightning bugs would flash on the lawn
like paparazzi shots of stars. The crickets would chant.
If I were the past, I'd go to the drive-in in the trunk of a car.
We'd laugh.
We'd drink Peppermint Schnapps and build a bonfire
in the back of the lot. If I were the past, we'd get naked
and roll in the grass.

II

If I were the past,
I would be driving a cherry Mercury. The autumn leaves
and the car would be like fire on the blacktop.
We'd drink a lot and play euchre in the burnout room.
We'd order pizza
and head south with our hair down
around our knees. Jerry Lee is rolling over Beethoven
and Bob Dylan is electrified
to rock the Aquarium. The Vietnam War is steady
on the radio and in our minds. Our spirits are heavy and wet
as the first flakes of falling snow. Our luck has run out,
we've won the lottery
to kill. We've been ordered by Nixon to MoTown
for a lesson in claustrophobia. I can't sleep.
I am accosted by honking cars and stark concrete
where the denizens are cold as thieves or whores
in wait for innocence. We are bluntly told
to follow the arrows and shut our mouths.
They wear white jackets
and stick fingers up our rectums. We are examined
and told we'd promptly lose our hair.
They accuse me of lying, so I am led and sequestered
to a white room where I am interrogated by a man that speaks
English interspersed with Russian. He smiles and acts friendly

in his attempt to outwit me. I am not a spy so I am not afraid.
I am naïve but not tricked. I have found my direction
around all manner of animals. Most of them run
when they catch your scent and this one in the end
acquiesces. I leave Detroit half blind and Classified
4F: useless 'til last resort. That's me
if I were the past.

JUSTICE

If I were the truth,
I might resolve or make the world's
problems. I might be heard and hard
to swallow at times. I might prove
guilt or innocence, depending on
the point of view. If I were the truth,
I might be a lie. I'd have to rely
on the reason why
you did or didn't
do it.

My Enemies

If I were a tombstone,
I'd stand erect
atop your grave.
I'd mark your death
and bear your name,
chiseled deep
across my chest.
I'd wear your epitaph
like a black tattoo.
My face would gleam
in a beam of sunlight.
I'd look at you
and feel nothing but stone.

Lost and Found

If I were a compass, I'd never lack sense
of direction. I could lead the way out of the maze
of confusion, drugs, and doubt. We'd always be certain
of where we stood. We'd hold our position. You'd see
right from wrong and never get lost or led astray
by wayward theories of ADHD and psychiatry.
You wouldn't wonder or wander if I were a compass.
We'd find our goals and purposes.
We would help our children
out of the abyss of pills for manic depression.
We could show them the path that leads to love and plenty
of discretion. If I were a compass, I'd never betray you.
If I were a compass, we'd find our way
back to the people we were meant to be.

HIGH HOPES

If I were a mountain,
I'd be rugged and tall
with my head in the clouds.
I'd be wild with rivers that whisper and roar;
I'd flourish with creatures,
forests, and storms. If I were a mountain,
my thunder would pound
hard as a hammer, crisp as the morn.
Come June, I'd flower
with poppy and glow. Come fall,
I'd showcase maple groves. I'd be orange and yellow,
red and bold. If I were a mountain,
I'd be capped in snow. I'd cradle a village
in a quaint meadow. I'd decorate Christmas
with evergreen spruce. If I were a mountain,
miners would sluice
their hopes and dreams from solitude.

The Universe

If I were a star,
I'd shine from the belt
of Orion. I'd be loyal to all
of my light-hearted friends. The night would become
devoid of darkness and hold forever
the dreams of men. I'd be the twinkle
vibrant and alive in their searching, distant eyes.
They'd have a hankering
to escape their prison planet Earth. If I were a star,
I'd grasp the hands of gravity and lift the chains
from atman lost. I would create
infinite time and infinite space for man to have
and then to grace. War would end and poverty would
be forgotten. Men would rocket
beyond their need for governing. No more George
Bush. Forget Obama. Forget the works. Men would rise
to greater heights then petty squabbles over votes. If
I were a star, I'd give to you the universe. Endless trillions
of planets like Earth, endless roles and endless purpose.
Our many lives would all add up
to being worth it.

Noah's Arc

If I were a pilot,
I'd fly backwards in time.
I'd become the past and future combined.
I'd get to Oswald before he shot John. NASA
would be perfectly fine. If I were a pilot, I'd be on a rocket
beyond the moon to distant planets. Earth
would heal her glaciers, the oceans would cool.
Whales would flourish, eagles soar, frogs would croak
while men explored, one by one, two by two, their
pristine blue Earth restored.

Handshake

If I were integrity,
I'd have an aura of confidence. I could
walk the street with my head on tight. I'd be whole
and well spoken. I could
own my rewards and accept my defeats. Nothing
and no one would get to me. I'd be
completely complete. If I were integrity,
I'd give credence my promise
and shake hands with God.

If I Were Done

If I were done, I could be
done in-
done in by ignorance,
done in by lies,
done in by violence,
done in by genocide.
If I were done, I could be
done from-
done from old age,
done from side effects,
done from silence,
done from neglect.
If I were done, I could be
done come-
done come Monsanto,
done come disaster,
done come George Soros,
done come here after.
If I were done, I could be
done for-
done for speaking out,
done for absurdity,
done for God,
done for eternity.
If I were done, I could be

done with-
done with poetry,
done with consent,
done with creation,
done with government.
If I were done, I could be
done with it all
but I ain't done yet.

FIRE

If I were a fire,
I'd burn at the root
of all that is cancerous to spirit and truth.
I'd leap at the lies; I'd render them mute.
I'd speak from their embers
with a blue-hot spark. If I were a fire,
I'd light up the dark. I would
hiss in the rain. I'd howl in the dell.
I'd judge true sinners
in the dungeons of Hell. If I were a fire,
I'd ravage and rage
through halls of injustice and houses that wage
destruction of freedoms guaranteed
by the constitution of the United States. I'd burn at the core
of corporate power and smoke out disciples
of covert war. If I were a fire, I'd smolder beneath
the coffers of Pfizer and Monsanto's keep.
I'd raise an inferno. I'd bellow disgrace.
If I were a fire, I'd burst
from the heart of the human race.

Social Mania

If I were the Internet
I'd have you look, look, look,
and buzz, buzz, buzz.
On Facebook,
I'd have you like, like, like.
On Wordpress
I'd have you follow, follow, follow.
On Twitter I'd have you love, love, love
to hate, hate, hate,
and tweet, tweet, tweet.
On YouTube you would
view, view, view.
On Pinterest you would pin, pin, pin,
and goo, goo, goo
on Google and do, do, do
on Instagram and buy, buy, buy
on Amazon.
For what, what, what
and why, why, why is the internet
worth a life spent?

Morning Commute

If I were stress,
I would
make you the ultimate
accident. I'd be there
just for you
on your morning commute.
I'd incite your anger
and your hyper
activity. I would
orchestrate
your schizophrenia
with two middle fingers
and obscenities. I'd cut
you off. I'd blare my horn.
I'd be your rage
bubbled up and let loose
like a genie escaped
from a whiskey bottle.
I'd grant your wish
with a deadly weapon.
I'd come unglued,
red faced and amok
as your high blood pressure.
pick up a gun
and squeeze the trigger.

Dirty Words

If I were a toothbrush,
I'd know my way
around your tongue.
I'd have knowledge
of how to avoid its deceit
and all your trash-
talking ways. I'd know
the ups and downs
of your teeth, how
their vulgar bite
involves your own
misdeeds. I'd seethe
and find reasons
for your obscenities with girls.
I'd remember how
to get my bristles up.
I wouldn't hide in the drawer
or idle around the sink.
If I were a toothbrush, I'd leap
off the counter and clean
your *bleeping* teeth.

Pretty Tight Buns

If I were a tennis shoe,
I'd get up every morning
to make you run.
It'd be my purpose,
It'd be my *om*. I'd make good sense
and use my tongue
if I were a tennis shoe. I'd bark like a dog
when I had to go out. I'd whine at the door
if you failed to get up. I'd soil your floor
if I were a tennis shoe. We would
go to the park and toe kick stones,
hard rock to the old Ramones, admire girls
with their pretty tight buns. You'd never get tired
of me as a friend. You'd never grow lazy
or fat in the end. If I were a tennis shoe,
you would tend to life
fit as a whistle and honed as a knife.

VOICE

If I were a canary,
I'd have the essence of song
written into my genes. I'd be
the golden one, the American
Idol of finches, with perfect tone
and perfect pitch. I'd warble in concert
with Adam Lambert, woo you
like Kelly Clarkson. I would
chortle with precision
to brighten your day. I would
harp for no reason,
pipe for pure pleasure,
and sing for release. If
I were a canary,
I'd raise my voice
far beyond the reach
of wings.

Food For Thought

If I were a sunflower,
I would seek to please
my farm, family, and friends
by keeping my head. I'd plan to stand out
in a crowded field. I'd be seductive
to colored birds and lady bugs. I'd fall in love
with the bumble of bees and the coo of doves.
I'd turn my face to worship the sun
and powder my cheeks
with pollens of sneezy
yellow fun. If I were a sunflower,
I would be ample and round. I'd grow
rotund. I'd secrete an aroma of gold perfume.
I'd have swirls and swirls of succulent seed.
If I were a sunflower, I'd promise to feed
our hungry world.

The Key

If I were a key,
I'd be a universal one.
I'd unlock doors to deep, dark secrets in the FBI.
I'd open and expose The World Bank
and its greed for money. I would crack the vaults
of the CIA. You could peek inside
the dirty files of giants like Chase and Novartis. You could
rattle the chains of the bad news boys. If I were a key,
I would make the punishment fit their crimes.
I could open minds and open hearts.
I could open eyes to all of the fruits
of observation. I could
enter your home or even your business,
steal and expose your identity like Amazon or Google,
but I wouldn't. If I were a key,
I'd be the key to honor and prosperity. I'd fit the mind
of ingenuity. I'd be the key
to interrelations, to negotiations. I'd open the nation
to a bigger game. I'd fit the world.

WOLF PACK MOON
for Ivan, Katie, and Otto

If I were a moon,
I'd take my place in the universe.
I'd orbit Earth. I'd sail above in the winter sky.
I'd raise the tide and make it slack. I'd guide your ship
from man to wife. I'd be your beacon
in the dark of night. Wolves would pack. Howls would echo
my audacity. I'd be okay. Monks would chant.
Tribes would dance and sing my praise.
If I were a moon, I'd give to you
fertility, men with heart and men with soul enough to woo
the arms of love and chivalry. They'd covet and sow
abundant seed. Wombs would swell, faces beam. I'd burst
with joy and the color of spring.

HOME

If I were a house,
I'd keep my windows
spic-and-span. All of my rooms
would be masculine
and feminine. I'd look out
more than in. I'd create an abundance
of soft spaces
for whimsical dreams and love's
gyrations. I'd be host to poetry
and folksy music. If I were a house,
I'd keep a ghost in the attic
and secrets in the basement.
I'd uncork a cask
of aged red wine. I wouldn't look
or feel confined. If I were a house,
I'd have a porch with a swing that creaks
and a pantry cooling pies.
I'd live in the country
away from the bustle and noise.

Touch and Grace

If I were a hand,
I could smooth a crease
from your worried face. I could
grasp what you hate
and hold it away
out of your reach. I could
glide you across the kitchen floor
while Neal Young strummed his blue guitar.
If I were a hand, I'd touch your waist.
I'd caress your cheek with touch and grace.
I'd pull you close and never let go.
If I were a hand, I'd lift your soul.

Respite

If I were a pail,
I'd have a big mouth.
I'd ring with the sound
of milking a cow. I'd clang
with the season of nuts. I'd peal like a bell
for the missus at supper. I'd holler you in
from the distant fields. I'd have water to bear
and food to thwart your hunger. If I were a pail,
I would go to the pig and the neighing horse
a little bit shy of full. In the empty of darkness,
I'd hang in the barn from a nail on a pole, seeking respite
from a long day and just a bucket away
from abuse.

Under The Weather

If I were snow,
I'd conspire with the wind.
We'd twirl and dance around your hat
and bite your ears and chin.
We'd nip your toes and make you stomp your feet.
I'd gather myself across the yard
and pile up around your car. If I were snow,
I'd work all night. In the morning I'd fill your TV screen.
I'd hang heavy on roof and eaves. The weight of me
would snap the trees. I'd cut the electricity, quick freeze
Facebook, Twitter and all that social media
in which you have faith. I'd block the roads. I'd keep your
children away from school. If I were snow,
you'd be stuck at home to fight the cold and flu.

Ghost

If I were a ghost,
I'd haunt your conscience.
I'd be a mirror to fathom
your improprieties. I'd be your karma,
I'd wear your clothes. I'd emit a hue
of putrid green. I'd have no feet and float
instead of walk into your room. I'd hover
creepily close to your head and sit erect with eager need
on the edge of your bed. Wantonly,
I'd watch you sleep. I'd reach
with empty sleeve to touch your neck.
I'd smell your breath and incite gooseflesh
down your back. I'd make you sweat. I'd make you jerk
and scream if I were a ghost.
I'd be your worst dream.

A Habit Good

If I had a habit good,
it would be to hold you,
heartfelt with passion, to drink of you
one sip at a time like fruity Merlot
or a Beaujolais. If I had a habit good,
I'd overindulge. I'd drink too much
and off would slip your shoes. I'd fondle and kiss
your perfect toes. My hands would go
wanderlust like gypsy sparrows or mourning doves.
They'd warble and whisper over your skin
like feathery silk. If I had a habit good,
my heart would swell. My lips would pucker.
My breath would rise and fall in a sea
of sensual brine. I'd sail with you. I'd lose control.
If I had a habit good, I'd want it to be
all yours.

Heaven

If I were the sky,
I'd find my center
from which to reach out.
I'd reach to the farthest
reaches of self.
I'd expand and contract, bend
and refract
all the colors of the rainbow.
I'd be the greatest
sculptor of light. I'd be God's painter
and spread deep yellows
like butter on dawn. I'd coax mellow mauves
to spruce up dusk. You'd snap my photo
and chase my storms. At night I would
cradle the moon, Jupiter
and Mars. I'd fling bright stars
into swirls and arcs. I'd always be high.
I'd never come down.
I'd never need time to keep me around.
If I were the sky, I'd know my worth
If I were the sky, I'd rain Heaven on Earth.

THE PANTRY

If I were a jar,
I'd be filled to the brim
with agates of blue
and deep yellow
like cat's eye marbles.
If I were a jar,
I'd be full of motes
and rays of bright,
bright sunshine.
I'd be filled with blossoms
and bees gilded gold
with sweet, sweet pollen. I'd be
unbreakable as a cup
full of smiles. If I were a jar,
I'd be drunk on moonshine.
I'd butter your bread
with honey and berry
and color your lips with red,
red cherry. If I were a jar,
I'd open my lid
and spill the beans. I would
ask for your hands
to cradle my neck,
reach inside, and fondle the depths,
grasp the essence of all we hold.

A Grape Poet

If I were a grape
poet, I'd be dreamy and fat.
I'd hang around and brew
about wine, jelly, or jam.
I'd soak in the sun
naked all day. I'd be
free of wrinkles.
I wouldn't worry
about UVs
or depletion of salts.
I'd drink a lot of water
until Jesus showed up.
If I were a grape
poet, I'd choose to be green
but I wouldn't be less
if I were purple or black
or somewhere in between.
I'd live on a hill
with a panoramic view
of Crystalline Creek
and Red Clay Villa.
If I were a grape
poet, I'd be real sweet.
I'd kiss a lot of neighbors
and find a mate

to cuddle and love
if I were a grape
poet. I'd be forever grapeful.
I'd be forever true.
I'd live with high purpose
and good taste, too. I would
always stand up
for my bunch of grapes.

The Rock

If I were a rock,
I'd be el capitan. I'd dominate
the landscape with a stone face
and intimidation. I could
hurl men like sacks into submission. I could
catch your breath and push you to the edge
of adrenalin. If I were a rock,
I'd scrape the sky in Philadelphia. I'd echo
the proclamations of Benjamin Franklin,
Thomas Paine and the constitution. I'd raise a monument
to common sense and confine the Fed
to a dank cell in Alcatraz prison. If I were a rock,
I'd fit in your pocket, I'd be smooth in your hand
and fly in abundance when the socialists come
with teargas, bullets and handcuffs. If I were a rock,
I'd tumble from the walls of the fortresses built
too big to fail, and crumble
to dust.

The End

If I were the future,
I might be famous
or dead.
But how could I die
if I lived instead?
I'd be in the library.
I'd speak from a book.
I'd appear in your mind
when you went for a look.
These words that I write
could last forever.
If I were the future,
I'd survive in the past.

Afterword

Richard is currently at work on a new book of Poetry called *HeartWood*. This is a collection of poems devoted to matters of the heart where love waters run deep. Life is fulfilled and denied by its drink. New beginnings and new ends are always born from the heart of the wood.

Harvest Moon

I combed my fingers

through corn silk hair

picking watermelon

kisses

and the breeze

rippled

the deep pools

of liquid

flesh

intoxicating

as chardonnay.

The grapes hung

ripe

on the hills

and the valleys sloped
into shimmering gold
cantaloupe plains.

Beneath
the pumpkin moon
I sip and feast
in a canyon sweet
oasis
of frangipani
and peppermint.

From *HeartWood,* by Richard Rensberry. Projected date of publication: December 2015, by QuickTurtle Books®.

About the Author

Richard Rensberry is the co-author of four children's books. They include: *It's Black and White/A Turtle Quest for the Ages*, *The QuickTurtles Go to School*, *Wake's Day*, and *Wake Helps*. He is the author of three chapbooks of poetry: *Snow Angels*, *Love Water*, and *Butchering Suzanne*. His poetry appeared in several small press magazines in the 1980s and 1990s. In 1999 and the early 2000s, Richard concentrated on charity work as well as fine art painting and sculpture. He used his artwork in conjunction with creating a charity golf tournament to raise many thousands of dollars to educate children on the dangers of drugs. In 2012 Richard teamed up with The Monterey Peninsula Foundation's Birdies for Charity program and with a team of San Francisco 49er players, including Brent Jones and Harris Barton, they won $20,000 for drug education via the Chevron Shootout which is part of the AT&T Pebble Beach ProAm festivities. Richard continues to write, paint, sculpt, and help educate children.

www.ingramcontent.com/pod-product-compliance
Lightning Source LLC
Chambersburg PA
CBHW021156080526
44588CB00008B/366